To _____

From _____

Other books by Exley:
Daughters …   Missing You …
Mothers …   Sisters …
True Love …

Published simultaneously in 1996 by Exley Publications in Great Britain, and
Exley Giftbooks in the USA.

12 11 10 9 8 7 6 5 4 3

Border illustrations by Juliette Clarke
Copyright © Helen Exley

ISBN 1-85015-711-1

Edited and pictures selected by Helen Exley.
Designed by Pinpoint Design.
Picture research by P. A. Goldberg and J. M. Clift, Image Select, London.
Typeset by Delta, Watford.
Printed in China

Exley Publications Ltd, 16 Chalk Hill, Watford, Herts. WD1 4BN.
Exley Giftbooks, 232 Madison Avenue, Suite 1206, NY 10016, USA.

When Love is forever

QUOTATIONS SELECTED BY
*H*ELEN EXLEY

≡ EXLEY
NEW YORK • WATFORD, UK

[Love is] born with the pleasure of looking at each other, it is fed with the necessity of seeing each other, it is concluded with the impossibility of separation!

JOSÉ MARTÍ (1835-1895),
FROM "AMOR"

Not till the sun excludes you do I exclude you, not till the waters refuse to glisten for you and the leaves to rustle for you, do my words refuse to glisten and rustle for you.

WALT WHITMAN (1819-1892)

Long as I live, my heart will never vary
For no one else, however fair or good
Brave, resolute or rich, of gentle blood,
My choice is made, and I will have no other.

FRENCH POEM (15/16TH CENTURY)

I will follow thee
To the last gasp
with truth
and loyalty.

WILLIAM SHAKESPEARE (1564-1616)

The moon shall be a darkness,
The stars shall give no light,
If I ever prove false
To my heart's delight.

ANONYMOUS

I want you for always – days, years, eternities.

ROBERT SCHUMANN (1810-1856),
TO CLARA WIECK

I would like to go through life side by side
with you, telling you more and more until
we grew to be one being together until the
hour should come for us to die.

JAMES JOYCE (1882-1941),
IN A LETTER TO HIS WIFE NORA

Grow old along with me!
the best is yet to be.

ROBERT BROWNING (1812-1889),
FROM "RABBI BEN EZRA"

… each day I love
you more,
Today more than
yesterday and
less than
tomorrow.

ROSEMONDE GERARD,
FROM "L'ETERNELLE CHANSON"

Treasure the love you receive above all. It will
survive long after your gold and good health
have vanished.

OG MANDINO

Love is absolute loyalty. People fade, looks
fade, but loyalty never fades.

SYLVESTER STALLONE, b.1946

Love, all alike, no season knows, nor clime,
Nor hours, days, months, which are the rags
of time.

JOHN DONNE (1572-1631),
FROM "THE SUN RISING"

Brief is life but long is love.

ALFRED, LORD TENNYSON (1809-1892)

How pretty romance is – like silk shot
through with gold – delicate as gossamer.
Love is sturdier stuff. Survives the hardest
wear. Can be scrubbed and stitched and
patched through an entire lifetime – and
flow more brightly with every passing year.

PAM BROWN, b.1928

The countless generations
Like Autumn leaves go by:
Love only is eternal,
Love only does not die...

HARRY KEMP,
FROM "THE PASSING FLOWER"

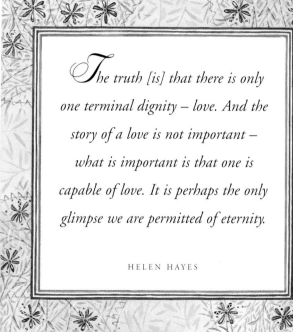

$\mathcal{T}$he truth [is] that there is only one terminal dignity – love. And the story of a love is not important – what is important is that one is capable of love. It is perhaps the only glimpse we are permitted of eternity.

HELEN HAYES

Without you, dearest dearest I couldn't see or hear or feel or think – or live – I love you so and I'm never in all our lives going to let us be apart another night. It's like begging for mercy of a storm or killing Beauty or growing old, without you. I want to kiss you so – and in the back where your dear hair starts and your chest – I love you – and I can't tell you how much....

ZELDA FITZGERALD (1900-1948),
IN A LETTER TO HER HUSBAND
F. SCOTT FITZGERALD

I love you, it's almost too wonderful
(to me) to say; but I want to say it and
I am saying IT: I love you: and we'll
always keep each other alive. We can
never do nothing at all now but that
both of us know all about it. You can
do anything & be anything, so long as
it's with me.

DYLAN THOMAS (1914-1953),
FROM A LETTER TO HIS WIFE-TO-BE,
CAITLIN MCNAMARA

To hold her in my arms against the twilight and be her comrade for ever – this was all I wanted so long as my life should last....
And this, I told myself with a kind of wonder, this was what love was: this consecration, this curious uplifting, this sudden inexplicable joy, and this intolerable pain....

ANONYMOUS

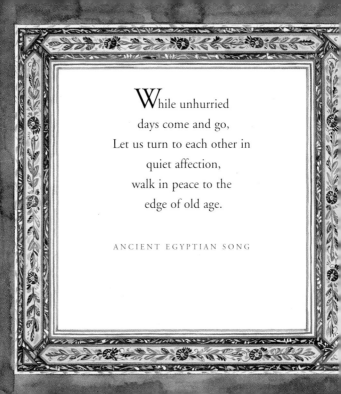

While unhurried
days come and go,
Let us turn to each other in
quiet affection,
walk in peace to the
edge of old age.

ANCIENT EGYPTIAN SONG

Oh, the head lies on the pillow–
twenty, thirty, forty years.
The hair that was brown goes grey,
then white.

But all the time the love increases.
To see the head there all those years
is itself a charm against the things
of night!

GAVIN EWART (1916-1995)

There is nothing more lovely in life than the union of two people whose love for one another has grown through the years from the small acorn of passion to a great rooted tree. Surviving all vicissitudes, and rich with its manifold branches, every leaf holding its own significance.

VITA SACKVILLE-WEST
(1892-1962)

When two souls, which have sought each other
for however long in the throng, have finally
found each other, when they have seen that they
are matched, are in sympathy and compatible, in
a word, that they are alike, there is then
established for ever between them a union, fiery
and pure as they themselves are, a union which
begins on earth and continues for ever in heaven.
This union is love, true love, such as in truth very
few men can conceive of, that love which is a
religion, which deifies the loved one, whose life
comes from devotion and passion, and for which
the greatest sacrifices are the sweetest delights.

VICTOR HUGO (1802-1885)

the quiet thoughts
of two people a long time in love
touch lightly
like birds nesting in each other's warmth
you will know them by their laughter
but to each other
they speak mostly through their solitude
if they find themselves apart
they may dream of sitting undisturbed
in each other's presence
of wrapping themselves warmly
in each other's easy

HUGH PRATHER, b.1938,
FROM "NOTES ON LOVE AND COURAGE"

The heart that loves is always young.

You are always new.
The last of your kisses was ever the sweetest;
the last smile the brightest; the last
movement the gracefullest.

JOHN KEATS (1795-1821),
TO FANNY BRAWNE

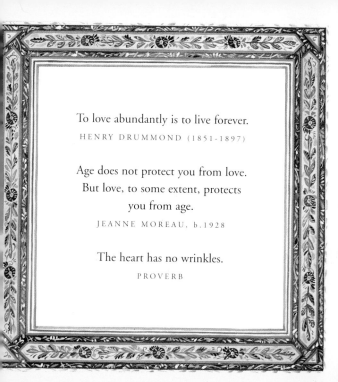

To love abundantly is to live forever.

HENRY DRUMMOND (1851-1897)

Age does not protect you from love.
But love, to some extent, protects
you from age.

JEANNE MOREAU, b.1928

The heart has no wrinkles.

PROVERB

I add my breath to your breath
That our days may be long in the earth
That the days of our people may be long
That we may be one person
That we may finish our roads together

KERES INDIAN SONG

FROM "A RED, RED ROSE"

As fair art thou, my bonnie lass,
So deep in love am I;
And I will love thee still, my dear,
Till a' the seas gang dry. –

Till a' the seas gang dry, my dear,
And the rocks melt wi' the sun:
I will love thee still, my dear,
While the sands o' life shall run.

ROBERT BURNS (1759-1796)

Until you're a hundred,
Until I'm ninety-nine,
Together
Until white hair grows

JAPANESE FOLK SONG

Love is something eternal – the aspect may
change, but not the essence.

VINCENT VAN GOGH (1853-1890)

You are wandering in the deep field

That backs on to the room I used to

work in

And from time to time

You look up to see if I am watching you

To this day

Your arms are full of the wild flowers

You were most in love with.

IAN HAMILTON

*W*e have lived and loved together
Through many changing years,
We have shared each other's gladness
And wept each other's tears.
And let us hope the future,
As the past has been will be:
I will share with thee my sorrows,
And thou thy joys with me.

CHARLES JEFFERYS (1807-1865),
FROM "WE HAVE LIVED AND LOVED
TOGETHER"

She has given me that perfect rest of heart and
mind of whose existence I had never
so much as dreamed before she came to
me, which springs out of assured oneness of
hope and sympathy – and which, for
me, means life and success. Above all she has
given me herself to live for! Her arms
are able to hold me up against the world: her eyes
are able to charm away every care; her
words are my solace and inspiration and
all because her love is my life....

THOMAS WOODROW WILSON
(1856-1924), PRESIDENT OF THE UNITED
STATES, OF HIS WIFE ELLEN

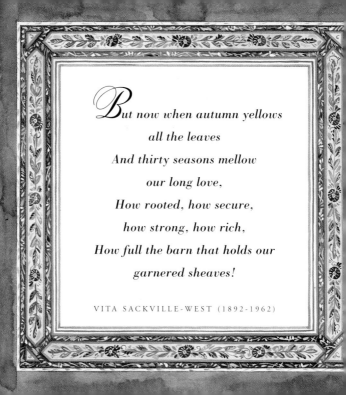

But now when autumn yellows
all the leaves
And thirty seasons mellow
our long love,
How rooted, how secure,
how strong, how rich,
How full the barn that holds our
garnered sheaves!

VITA SACKVILLE-WEST (1892-1962)

As I said, I don't fear Death, but I do fear being left without Tom for he has been my stay, my right hand, and comfort for forty-seven years. We often discuss our parting, and he fears it more than I, if that is possible. I say to him: "When I go, take all the money and buy yourself a yacht and sail the seas," for this has been his lifetime's desire, but he just looks at me as if to say, "Don't be silly."

What shall I do when he goes?

Only God knows.

CATHERINE COOKSON, b.1906

If I do not return, my dear Sarah, never forget how much I loved you, nor that when my last breath escapes me on the battlefield, it will whisper your name.… "If the dead can come back to this earth and flit unseen around those they loved, I shall always be near you; in the gladdest days and in the darkest nights … *always always*, and if there be a soft breeze upon your cheek, it shall be my breath, as the cool air fans your throbbing temple, it shall be my spirit.…"

MAJOR SULLIVAN BALLOU, IN A LETTER TO HIS WIFE, JUST ONE WEEK BEFORE THE FIRST BATTLE OF BULL RUN, IN WHICH MAJOR BALLOU WAS KILLED

In the opinion of the world, marriage ends all, as it does in a comedy. The truth is precisely the opposite: it begins all.

ANNE SOPHIE SWETCHINE

Love is supposed to start with bells ringing and go downhill from there. But it was the opposite for me. There's an intense connection between us, and as we stayed together, the bells rang louder.

LISA NIEMI

Husband and wife come to look alike at last.

OLIVER WENDELL HOLMES (1809-1894), FROM "THE PROFESSOR AT THE BREAKFAST TABLE"

A good leg will fall; a straight back will stoop; a black beard will turn white; a curled pate will grow bald, a fair face will wither; a full eye will wax hollow; but a good heart, Kate, is the sun and the moon; or rather the sun and not the moon; for it shines bright and never changes, but keeps his course truly.

WILLIAM SHAKESPEARE (1564-1616)

I have lived long enough to know that the
evening glow of love has its own riches and
splendour.

BENJAMIN DISRAELI (1804-1881)

No spring nor summer beauty hath
such grace
As I have seen in one autumnal face.

JOHN DONNE (1572-1631)

Let my love find its strength
in the service of day,
its peace in the union of night.

RABINDRANATH TAGORE (1861-1941),
FROM "FIREFLIES"

I love her with a love as still
As a broad river's peaceful might,
Which by high tower and lowly mill,
Seems following its own wayward will,
And yet doth ever flow aright.

JAMES RUSSELL LOWELL (1819-1891)

And our love found ways of speaking
What words cannot say,
Till a hundred nests gave music,
And the east was gray.

FREDERIC LAWRENCE KNOWLES
(1869-1905), "A MEMORY"

Though I am old with wandering
Through hollow lands and hilly lands,
I will find out where she has gone,
And kiss her lips and take her hands;
And walk among long dappled grass,
And pluck till time and times are done,
The silver apples of the moon,
The golden apples of the sun.

WILLIAM BUTLER YEATS (1865-1939),
FROM "THE SONG OF THE WANDERING
AENGUS"

Grandmother had won Grandfather by slipping notes into his boots as he mounted guard at Horse Guards Parade at the turn of the century. Their relationship continued on this somewhat eccentric level until he died. He was a tall, straight-backed, gentle man, full of quiet humour and with a capacity for amiable frolic. Grandmother was a darting terrier to his placid Great Dane. He regarded her all their life together with a kindly but slightly puzzled tolerance, and a deep affection. She outlived him by twenty years, outwardly as stubborn, as busy, as given to mild scallywaggery as ever – but in her heart simply marking time. I do not think he really settled down to Eternity until she joined him.

PAM BROWN, b.1928

Sensual pleasure passes and vanishes in the
twinkling of an eye, but the friendship
between us, the mutual confidence, the
delights of the heart, the enchantment of
the soul, these things do not perish and
can never be destroyed. I shall love you
until I die.

VOLTAIRE (1694-1778),
TO MME. DENIS

He was comforted by one of the simpler
emotions which some human beings are
lucky enough to experience. He knew
when he died he would be watched by
someone he loved.

NOEL ANNAN ON E. M. FORSTER

The ancients held, it is said, that each human being is but half of a perfect unit; and that the divine healing of life's wounds comes only when one has the rare good fortune to meet the half of himself. Then are both, as Plato writes, "smitten with a friendship in a wondrous way": and these continue to be friends through life.

J. C. DIER

$\mathcal{L}$et the young make up their love songs,
about which subject they are securely
ignorant.
Let them look into eyes that mirror
themselves. Let them groan and ululate
their desire into a microphone. Let them
shout their proclamations over the tannoy
– a whisper is enough for us.

GEORGE BRUCE, FROM "LOVE IN AGE"

The white wine of youth is beautiful – light
and bright and fresh as the air of Spring.
But age brings subtlety, depth – a marvellous
maturity.
Brief loves are piquant – but the love that
lasts a lifetime grows richer with the years.

PAM BROWN, b.1928

Is not old wine wholesomest, old pippins
toothsomest, old wood burn brightest, old
linen was whitest? Old soldiers, sweethearts,
are surest, and old lovers are soundest.

JOHN WEBSTER (c.1580-c.1625),
FROM "WESTWARD HO"

To see a young couple loving each other is no wonder; but to see an old couple loving each other is the best sight of all.

WILLIAM MAKEPEACE THACKERAY
(1811-1863)

The love we have in our youth is superficial compared to the love that an old man has for his old wife.

WILL DURANT (1885-1981)

An old man loved is winter with flowers.

GERMAN PROVERB

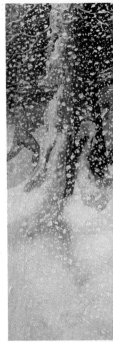

There is no grief, no sorrow, no despair, no languor,

no dejection, no dismay, no absence scarcely can there

be, for those who love as we do.

WILLIAM WORDSWORTH (1770-1850)

Love bears all things, believes all things,

hopes all things, endures all things.

Love never ends.

1 CORINTHIANS 13:7

But love is a durable fire

In the mind ever burning;

Never sick, never old, never dead

From itself never turning.

SIR WALTER RALEIGH (1552-1618)

Time flies, suns rise, and shadows fall –

Let them go by, for love is over all.

FOUND ON A SUNDIAL

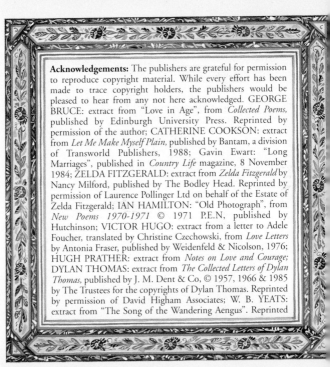

Acknowledgements: The publishers are grateful for permission to reproduce copyright material. While every effort has been made to trace copyright holders, the publishers would be pleased to hear from any not here acknowledged. GEORGE BRUCE: extract from "Love in Age", from *Collected Poems,* published by Edinburgh University Press. Reprinted by permission of the author; CATHERINE COOKSON: extract from *Let Me Make Myself Plain,* published by Bantam, a division of Transworld Publishers, 1988; Gavin Ewart: "Long Marriages", published in *Country Life* magazine, 8 November 1984; ZELDA FITZGERALD: extract from *Zelda Fitzgerald* by Nancy Milford, published by The Bodley Head. Reprinted by permission of Laurence Pollinger Ltd on behalf of the Estate of Zelda Fitzgerald; IAN HAMILTON: "Old Photograph", from *New Poems 1970-1971* © 1971 P.E.N, published by Hutchinson; VICTOR HUGO: extract from a letter to Adele Foucher, translated by Christine Czechowski, from *Love Letters* by Antonia Fraser, published by Weidenfeld & Nicolson, 1976; HUGH PRATHER: extract from *Notes on Love and Courage;* DYLAN THOMAS: extract from *The Collected Letters of Dylan Thomas,* published by J. M. Dent & Co, © 1957, 1966 & 1985 by The Trustees for the copyrights of Dylan Thomas. Reprinted by permission of David Higham Associates; W. B. YEATS: extract from "The Song of the Wandering Aengus". Reprinted